Planets

Neptune

Dash!
LEVELED READERS
An Imprint of Abdo Zoom • abdobooks.com

3

Dash!
LEVELED READERS

Level 1 – Beginning
Short and simple sentences with familiar words or patterns for children who are beginning to understand how letters and sounds go together.

Level 2 – Emerging
Longer words and sentences with more complex language patterns for readers who are practicing common words and letter sounds.

Level 3 – Transitional
More developed language and vocabulary for readers who are becoming more independent.

abdobooks.com

Published by Abdo Zoom, a division of ABDO, PO Box 398166, Minneapolis, Minnesota 55439.
Copyright © 2019 by Abdo Consulting Group, Inc. International copyrights reserved in all countries.
No part of this book may be reproduced in any form without written permission from the publisher.
Dash!™ is a trademark and logo of Abdo Zoom.

Printed in the United States of America, North Mankato, Minnesota.
092018
012019

Photo Credits: iStock, NASA, Science Source, Shutterstock
Production Contributors: Kenny Abdo, Jennie Forsberg, Grace Hansen, John Hansen
Design Contributors: Dorothy Toth, Neil Klinepier

Library of Congress Control Number: 2018946202

Publisher's Cataloging in Publication Data

Names: Murray, Julie, author.
Title: Neptune / by Julie Murray.
Description: Minneapolis, Minnesota : Abdo Zoom, 2019 | Series: Planets |
    Includes online resources and index.
Identifiers: ISBN 9781532125300 (lib. bdg.) | ISBN 9781641856751 (pbk) |
    ISBN 9781532126321 (ebook) | ISBN 9781532126833 (Read-to-me ebook)
Subjects: LCSH: Neptune (Planet)--Juvenile literature. | Neptune (Planet)--
    Exploration--Juvenile literature. | Planets--Juvenile literature. | Solar system--
    Juvenile literature.
Classification: DDC 523.48--dc23

Table of Contents

Neptune

Earth

Mercury

Sun

Venus

Jupiter

Uranus

Neptune

Mars

Saturn

Neptune is the farthest
plane from the sun. It has
14 moons and 5 rings.

Neptune's surface is made up of gas and liquid. The **atmosphere** consists of helium, hydrogen, and methane.

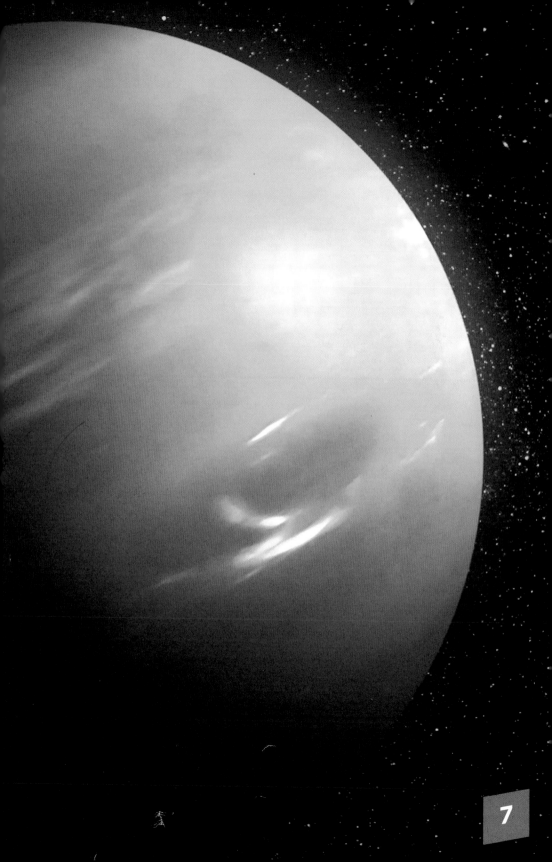

Core

Neptune's internal core is made up of ice and rock. Its middle layer is a thick liquid that can reach 5,000 °F (2,760 °C).

It takes Neptune 165 Earth years to **orbit** the sun. That is a long year! The planet spins as it moves. It takes 16 hours, or one day on Neptune, to complete one rotation.

Neptune is tilted on its **axis**. This creates seasons on the planet. Because of its long **orbit**, each season lasts for more than 40 years!

Stormy Planet

It is stormy on Neptune. Violent clouds of gas swirl. Winds can blow up to 1,500 mph (2,414 kph)! Dark spots seen on the planet are giant storms. Some storms are the size of Earth.

Neptune is one of the coldest planets. Its average temperature is -346 °F (-210 °C).

17

Neptune Missions

Voyager 2 is the only spacecraft to visit Neptune. It flew by the planet in 1989. It took measurements and photos of Neptune's **atmosphere**, moons, and rings.

The **Hubble Space Telescope** has sent updated photos of Neptune to Earth. Another spacecraft may be sent to study the planet in the next 25 years.

- It takes more than 4 hours for the sun's light to reach Neptune. That is because it is 3 billion miles (4.8 billion km) from the sun!

- Neptune is so big that 58 Earths could fit inside it.

- Neptune looks blue in color. That is because the methane gas absorbs the red light and reflects the blue light back into space.

Glossary

atmosphere – the gases surrounding the earth or other planets in our solar system.

axis – a real or imaginary line through the center of an object, around which the object turns.

Hubble Space Telescope – a space telescope that was built by NASA and launched into Earth orbit in 1990. It observes and takes photographs, and transmits the information back to Earth.

orbit – a curved path in which a planet, or other space object, moves in a circle around another body.

Index

Online Resources

Booklinks
NONFICTION NETWORK
FREE! ONLINE NONFICTION RESOURCES

To learn more about Neptune, please visit
abdobooklinks.com. These links are routinely
monitored and updated to provide the most current
information available.